CHAMPIONS OF OUR PLANET

Vaishali Batra

Illustrated by **Marco Marella**

OXFORD
UNIVERSITY PRESS

I live in Auckland, New Zealand, with my husband, two teenage sons and a puppy named Rover. There is nothing I enjoy more than exploring New Zealand's stunning landscape and marvelling at the fragile beauty of nature. Whether I choose a path through a busy city or a quiet reserve, I am always reminded of how connected humans are to nature.

As the author of several children's books, I research and write about our wonderful planet, the dangers it faces and how each one of us can play a part in caring for it, so we can leave it better than we found it.

Vaishali Batra

Contents

The glossary

Some words in this book are in **bold**. When you read a **bold** word, think about what it means. If you don't know, you can look it up in the glossary at the end of the book.

Caring for the Planet – Our Home

We live on a unique and wonderful planet. It has many natural resources such as water, air, soil, minerals, fuels, plants and animals. We are able to use many of these resources. But what do you think would happen if we used our planet's resources for our needs and forgot to think about what this means for the rest of life on the planet?

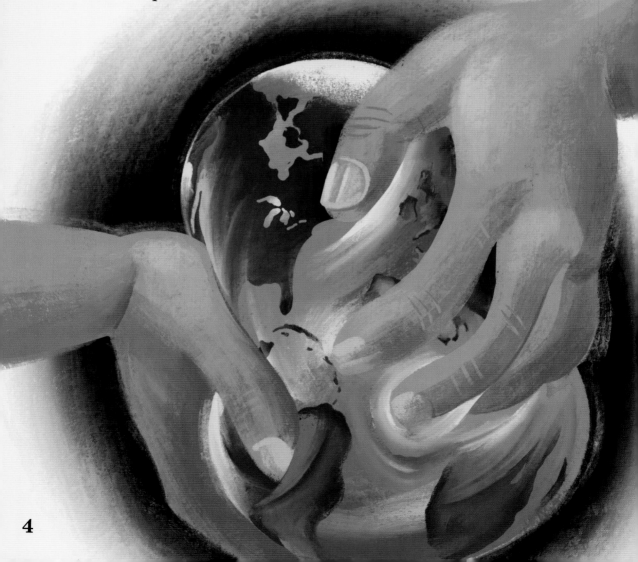

Human impact on our planet

Almost everything we do impacts our planet. Some of our actions, such as planting **native** trees and using resources carefully, help to keep nature in balance. But some of our actions, such as littering, hunting animals and cutting down forests, are very destructive.

These actions affect humans too – we depend on the planet as much as it depends on us. We depend on it for fuel. And like all other animals, we depend on it for food and clean water.

Each of us has a responsibility to be a guardian of our planet. Some of us may believe that we are powerless to make a difference. You may feel discouraged if you think that only adults can change the world. This isn't true. You can make a difference, too.

Have you heard about the work Greta Thunberg has done to bring the problems facing our planet today to the world's attention? Around the world, there are many children who have seen a problem and thought of a way to solve it. You may not have heard of them, but they have shown the world a better way of doing things. Some of them have helped other people rethink what they were doing to the planet. All of their ideas and actions have made a positive impact.

Richard Turere

Richard Turere, a young boy from Kenya, made a simple invention that solved a significant problem. It helped his family, and it has also helped lions across Africa.

FACT FILE

All species in nature, including humans, depend on one another. So when an animal becomes extinct, it can affect other species. For example, predators help to control the populations of the animals they prey upon. When a predator becomes extinct, the animals it preys upon may multiply unchecked, and in time, they may run out of food and become extinct themselves. It is very important to protect endangered species to keep nature in balance.

wolf

elk

grass

grass

beaver

A healthy food chain

When wolves prey on elk, beavers are able to live in the same area.

Impact of extinction on food chain

When wolves are wiped out in the area, the elk numbers rise. The elk eat more food and the beavers are squeezed out.

FACT FILE

One of the reasons animals become endangered is because their **habitat** is destroyed. When people take land away from animals to make space for expanding towns and cities, the animals do not have enough space to live or enough food to eat. Many species become endangered because people hunt them to eat and sometimes for sport. Other animal species suffer when people bring farm animals to graze in their habitat.

One way of helping endangered species is to leave them undisturbed in protected areas. These areas are called nature reserves or national parks.

Nairobi National Park in Kenya provides a safe home to a large variety of wildlife including black rhinos, zebras, lions, leopards, cheetahs, hyenas, buffaloes and giraffes.

The park is fenced on three sides. Its southern boundary is open to allow herds of herbivores, such as zebras, to move between the park and the nearby grasslands in search of **pastures**. However, the open boundary also allows predators, such as lions, to venture out of the park and prey on cows and sheep, especially at night.

Richard Turere lived with his family in Kitengela, an area bordering the southern side of Nairobi National Park. Like other families in the community, Richard's family depended on raising cattle for food, clothing and shelter.

When Richard was nine years old, he began to help look after the family's cattle. He guarded them during the day, but he couldn't watch them at night while he slept. During the night, lions would sneak up from the open boundary of the national park to feed on the family's cattle. Richard's family would lose up to nine cattle a week.

Because the community depended on the cattle for their **livelihood**, losing them to the lions was a huge problem. Sometimes, they gathered in groups to attack and kill the preying lions. However, this meant the already low number of lions in the park became lower still.

Lions are at risk of extinction. Kenya has been losing about 100 lions each year for the past few years.

Richard began to think about ways to solve
the problem by scaring the lions away. At first, he made
a scarecrow, but this didn't help, as the lions ignored the scarecrow
and continued to attack the cattle night after night.

Next, Richard built a dark shed, so the lions couldn't see inside the cattle
pen. This didn't work either because the lions could still smell the cattle in
the dark.

One evening when the sun went down, Richard walked around the
cattle pen with a torch. As long as he kept watch, the lions didn't come
close. But when he went to sleep, they crept up to the pen to prey on the
cattle. Richard figured out that the lions would only stay away as long as
someone was walking around with a light.

Richard decided to invent a way to trick the lions into believing someone was walking around with a torch. He fitted LED (light-emitting diode) bulbs onto poles around the pen. The bulbs were wired to an old car battery and a box with switches. When he turned on the switch, the lights flickered on and off all through the night – and the lions stayed away! In this clever way, Richard managed to keep his family's cattle safe at night.

Richard's LED lights mimicked the flickering of his torch moving around, so he did not have to stay up all night and keep watch.

Richard learned about electronics on his own. He took apart some household appliances, such as a radio, and then set about fixing them.

Richard's idea helped his family by protecting the cattle from the lions. Equally, it helped keep the lions safe from humans. Over time, Richard installed similar lights around the cattle pens of other families in the community. His invention became known as Lion Lights. He set up his Lion Lights in hundreds of homes.

Afterwards, Richard improved his invention. He used his interest in electronics to come up with new ideas. Later, he made a wind turbine to power the light system. This was useful on cloudy days when there was little sunlight to power the lights.

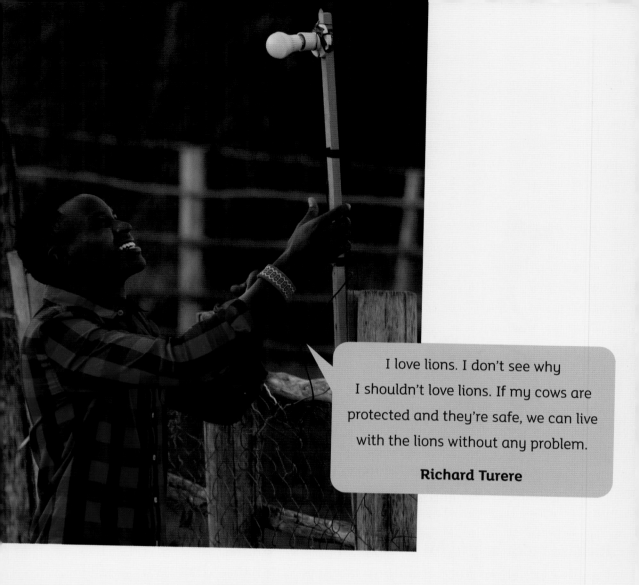

> I love lions. I don't see why I shouldn't love lions. If my cows are protected and they're safe, we can live with the lions without any problem.
>
> **Richard Turere**

Even ten years later, Richard's flashing lights continued to work throughout the night to protect the endangered lions from people as well as protecting the community's cattle from the lions.

Because of his invention, Richard got a **scholarship** to one of the best schools in Kenya. He also gave a talk at a TED (Technology, Entertainment, Design) conference. It has been watched online by millions of people.

Ryan Hreljac

Ryan Hreljac, a young boy from Canada, decided to help people who were working to solve the problem of water shortage. He helped raise money to build a well in Uganda.

The problem – shortage of fresh water

Water covers about 70% of our planet, but most of this water is unavailable for use. That's because only 2.5% of it is **fresh water**, out of which almost 70% is frozen in the ice caps covering Antarctica and Greenland. Only about 1% of the fresh water on our planet is available for us to use in our homes, farms and factories.

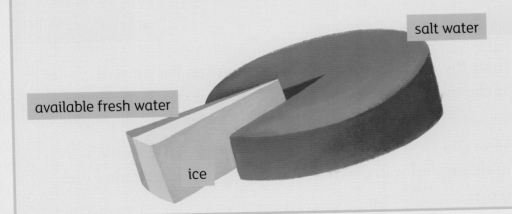

salt water

available fresh water

ice

Using and drinking unsafe water is a major health hazard. It causes diseases and even deaths, but often people have no other option but to drink unsafe water.

The growth of the human population over the years has created a huge demand for the limited amount of available fresh water. Furthermore, patterns of weather are changing around the world – causing shortages in some places and floods in others. In many parts of the world, rivers, lakes and underground water sources are drying up or becoming too polluted to use.

When Ryan Hreljac was six years old, his teacher at school talked about how people in some parts of the world did not have access to clean water. Ryan was surprised to learn that some people who live in rural communities had to walk for hours, often several times a day, to fetch water for their families. Even children would miss out on time learning at school. Often, the water they got was dirty, polluted with waste and unsafe to use.

He also learned that people in many communities were working hard to solve the problem. He decided he wanted to help them.

At first, Ryan thought about offering $70, an amount he thought would help build a well to provide clean water. When he asked his parents for money, they suggested he do extra chores around the house to earn it. In addition to his regular chores such as making his bed and clearing the table, he started doing other tasks – he washed windows, vacuumed his home and shovelled snow. It took Ryan four months to raise $70, only to find out that building a well would cost nearly $2000! But he did not give up.

Ryan decided he would do more chores to collect enough money. He had set his mind on building a well that would provide safe and clean water.

He encouraged his classmates to get involved with raising money too. He began **fundraising** in the community and making speeches to spread awareness about the importance of clean water. It took several months for Ryan to collect nearly $2000.

He sent the money to a charity that was trying to solve the freshwater problem in some countries in Africa by working with the people living there. The charity used the money to buy tools. With the tools, the local people were able to drill a well near a school in Agweo, Uganda.

Ryan's teacher decided to teach her pupils more about life in Uganda. She paired up her pupils with Ugandan children from Angolo Primary School – the school near the well. Ryan was paired with Jimmy Akana, a young orphan. They wrote each other letters and shared glimpses of their lives with each other.

When Ryan visited Uganda the following year, he was able to meet his friend Jimmy and see the well. Engraved on the side of the well were the words:

Ryan's Well
Funded by Ryan H.
For the community of Angolo
Primary School

The well built near Angolo Primary School continues to provide water to thousands of people.

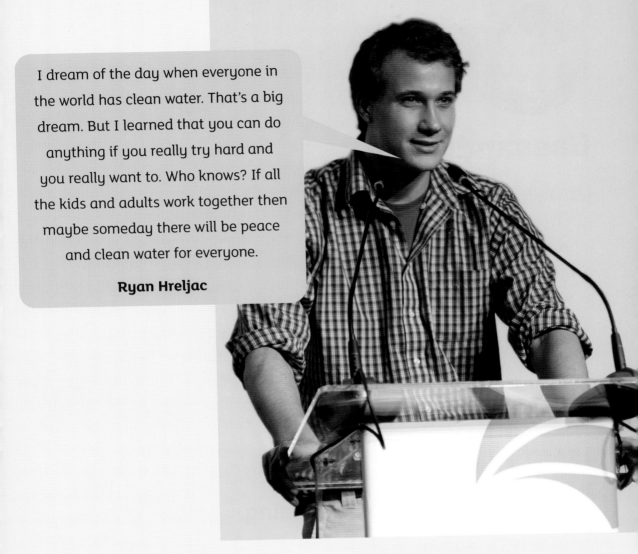

> I dream of the day when everyone in the world has clean water. That's a big dream. But I learned that you can do anything if you really try hard and you really want to. Who knows? If all the kids and adults work together then maybe someday there will be peace and clean water for everyone.
>
> **Ryan Hreljac**

Ryan founded a charity called Ryan's Well Foundation the following year. The charity works alongside locals to construct clean water projects across the world. Over the years, the charity has raised funds and supported clean water projects in several African countries, as well as Mexico, Haiti, India, Guatemala and Guyana.

As an adult today, Ryan makes speeches to encourage people to help solve the problem of fresh water shortage around the world.

Cassandra Lin

Cassandra Lin, a young girl from the USA, started a project that helped people in her community as well as the environment.

FACT FILE

The problem – global warming

Scientists have observed that temperatures all over the world are increasing slowly. Warmer temperatures can cause big changes to land and the oceans. Many places are experiencing **droughts**. Without enough water, plants cannot grow and animals and people suffer because there is little water to drink or plants to eat.

Ice in the Arctic and Antarctic is melting due to these increasing temperatures. In the Arctic, this affects animals such as polar bears, which rely on ice as part of their habitat. The ice melting in the Antarctic is making sea levels rise, which threatens islands and coastal areas with flooding.

FACT FILE

Scientists have shown that humans contribute to global warming when they use **fossil fuels**. Fossil fuels such as coal, oil and natural gas are found underground and people use them as a source of energy. Around the world, most electrical power comes from power plants that burn coal or natural gas, and most cars run on fuel that comes from oil. But burning fossil fuels creates a problem for the planet in the form of **greenhouse gases**, such as carbon dioxide. Greenhouse gases in our atmosphere stop heat from escaping and result in warmer temperatures on Earth. This leads to further problems such as melting ice, rising sea levels and more extreme weather, including floods and droughts.

The sun provides heat.
The atmosphere traps some heat.

Greenhouse gases in the atmosphere trap extra heat.

Cassandra Lin lived with her family in Westerly, a coastal town in Rhode Island. When Cassandra was eight years old, she learned about global warming at school. She learned that one of the main causes of the problem was the burning of fossil fuels.

Cassandra became worried that if global warming continued, it was possible that parts of her coastal town could eventually be submerged underwater. She decided she needed to do something about it. She got together with a group of friends to find a way to solve this problem. The group brainstormed ideas and researched information about global warming.

Cassandra and her friends also learned that when people pour waste oil down the drain, it can pollute the oceans. They discovered that waste cooking oil can be turned into a fuel called biodiesel. Biodiesel is cleaner than other kinds of fuel because it gives off less carbon dioxide when burned. And it can be used to heat homes.

Global warming is made worse by continued use of fossil fuels ...

... but it can be slowed down by using cleaner fuels, such as biodiesel, instead.

One day Cassandra read an article in the newspaper about a local charity which was working to help people who could not afford to heat their homes in winter. She remembered what she had learned about biodiesel and came up with a simple solution.

Cassandra's plan was to collect waste oil, convert it into biodiesel and distribute that fuel to families who needed it.

She and her friends started the project by spreading the message about global warming. They handed out flyers and kitchen calendars and made presentations in the community.

They asked the town council to set up a container at the local waste station where residents could recycle their oil.

They asked local restaurants to donate their waste grease to be recycled into biodiesel.

They requested local **biofuel** companies to **refine** the collected waste oil to make biodiesel.

Cassandra's idea finally became Project TGIF – Turn Grease Into Fuel. Project TGIF collects grease from restaurants and homes, and supplies it to recycling centres so that it can be turned into biofuel.

Project TGIF brought together several groups and businesses – restaurants that donated used cooking oil, grease collectors that transported the oil, biofuel companies that processed it, and local charities that helped provide biodiesel to families in need.

COOKING OIL

Cassandra also worked to gather support for a law that would require all businesses to recycle their waste cooking oil. It is called the Used Cooking Oil Recycling Act, and became law in Rhode Island in 2014.

By encouraging the use of biodiesel to heat homes, Cassandra's project helped stop a large amount of carbon dioxide from entering the air. The project has also been able to donate the fuel to help hundreds of families to stay warm in the winter. Additionally, biofuel began to be used to power local school buses.

... a simple passion – in my case, the environment – can go a long way. I really believe that youth are the change-makers, the leaders of today and tomorrow.

Cassandra Lin

After a few years, Cassandra took her idea to other neighbouring communities in Rhode Island, Connecticut and Massachusetts. She has also developed a **toolkit**, which provides information for people to start similar projects in their communities. Cassandra's idea and hard work are producing positive results for the planet as well as for her local community.

Melati and Isabel Wijsen

Sisters Melati and Isabel Wijsen, from the Indonesian island of Bali, started a project to solve the island's problem of plastic pollution.

The problem – plastic pollution

Disposable plastic bags are convenient to use and readily available. Once used, they are usually discarded and add to piles of waste in **landfills**. In a landfill, plastic bags can take hundreds of years to break down. When waste plastic bags are exposed to sunlight, they break down into tiny bits that get mixed up in soil. These tiny plastics can harm plants.

FACT FILE

Plastic bags are lightweight, so when they are thrown away carelessly, they get blown into rivers and drains that flow into oceans. Birds and marine animals can mistake plastic bags for food. They can choke or get poisoned by swallowing the plastic.

Furthermore, plastic bags are made from resources such as petroleum and natural gas. Their production releases many harmful gases into the atmosphere. As a result, our planet suffers from their production as well as their disposal.

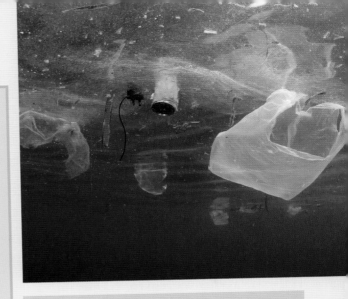

Scientists estimate there are currently hundreds of marine species at risk of extinction due to plastic pollution. In fact, if we don't stop the problem, there may be more plastic waste in our oceans than fish by 2050.

The dangers of plastic waste

Bali has some of the most beautiful beaches on our planet. But every year, a large amount of plastic waste washes up on the beaches. When sisters Melati and Isabel Wijsen were ten and twelve years old, they regularly found discarded plastic bags when they swam in the ocean. Along the beach there would be plastic waste strewn all around. When they played in the fields, they saw plastic bags clogging the gutters and piling up on the side of the road. Research told them that the island produced enough plastic waste each day to easily fill up a 14-storey building! The sisters decided to take action to stop it. But how could they get the people of Bali to say no to plastic bags?

The sisters were inspired by a lesson at school about the work of leaders who brought about big changes in the world. They began to spread the message online about the harmful effects of plastic pollution and began encouraging the use of alternatives to plastic. Their campaign was called Bye Bye Plastic Bags. They organized beach clean-ups and encouraged people to come along to help. Nearly 12 000 people joined their effort to pick up the plastic waste littered on Bali's beaches.

In 2017, Bali declared a "garbage emergency" across 6 kilometres of the island's beaches where 100 tonnes of rubbish was found.

To spread their message further, they started a petition online to stop the use, sale and production of plastics bags. They were able to collect hundreds of thousands of signatures. They took their petition to Bali's government, requesting action without delay. The girls' sincere efforts made news all around the country. Their campaign finally found success after six years, when they managed to convince the Bali government to ban all single-use plastics, including straws and **polystyrene**.

Melati and Isabel continue to discover new ways to combat the damage done by plastic waste and pollution. They are looking to find ways to make all plastics recyclable, compostable or reusable in the future. They have started a project that helps women in Bali's mountains earn extra income by learning how to make bags from donated, recyclable materials.

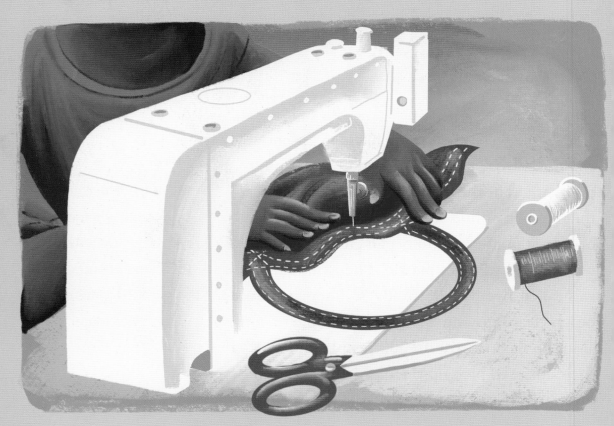

We didn't want to wait until we were older to stand up for what we believe in.

Melati and Isabel Wijsen

The sisters are working to spread the word in other countries, too. They give speeches explaining the importance of solving the problem of plastic pollution. Melati and Isabel have also made a handbook that guides other young people to start similar projects in their communities.

Over to You!

The children in this book used their ideas and learning to find a solution to some of the problems facing our planet. You too can contribute to conservation and caring for our planet's resources, so that all living things can benefit from them now and in the future.

What can you do to support conservation *right now*?

- Turn off lights and electronic devices when not in use.
- Walk, ride a bike, **carpool** and use public transport.
- Turn off the tap while brushing your teeth.
- Take short showers.
- Recycle paper, aluminium cans, glass and plastic items.
- Plant trees.
- Use both sides of every sheet of paper.
- Take your own reusable bags when you go shopping.
- Carry reusable water bottles and food containers.

OFF

ON

Glossary

biofuel: fuel made from plants or waste material

carpool: groups of people travelling together by car

disposable: an article intended to be thrown away after use

droughts: long periods of time during which there is too little or no rainfall

extinct: no longer alive anywhere on the planet

fossil fuels: fuels such as coal, oil and natural gas, found in the earth

fresh water: water from lakes, rivers, snow and ice, which is not salty

fundraising: doing things to collect money for a purpose

greenhouse gases: gases in the atmosphere that trap heat

habitat: the place or environment where a plant or animal normally lives or grows

landfills: places where waste is buried under the ground

livelihood: a way of earning money in order to live

native: a plant or animal that originally grew or lived in a particular place

pastures: areas of land where animals feed on grass

polystyrene: a type of light plastic often used in food containers

refine: to make a substance pure by taking other substances out of it

scholarship: a free place at a top school, given as a kind of prize

species: groups of living things which are closely related and can breed together

toolkit: a set of resources

Index